THE
SCHOOL RECORDER
BOOK 1

For Descant Recorder REVISED EDITION

by the late E. PRIESTLEY, M.B.E., M.Ed., B.Sc., L.R.A.M.

and F. FOWLER M.B.E., L.T.C.L.

EJA Publications

Exclusive Distributors:
Music Sales Limited
14-15 Berners Street, London W1T 3LJ, UK.
Music Sales Pty Limited
20 Resolution Drive, Caringbah, NSW 2229, Australia.

Order No. EJ10015
ISBN 0-7119-5007-5

Foreword

When *The School Recorder Books* first appeared, nearly a quarter of a century ago, few schools in this country had groups or classes of recorder players, and very few people knew what recorders were.

Today thousands and thousands of children play recorders in schools throughout the world. The recorder has been accepted as a most suitable instrument for music making in schools. It is inexpensive; it is a serious musical instrument with its own repertoire; it combines well with voices and other musical instruments; it is fairly easy to play and a whole class can learn to play at the same time.

We feel that *The School Recorder Books* have played an important part in this growth of recorder playing.

In revising *The School Recorder Books* we have taken the opportunity of simplifying the early stages of playing in order to suit the much younger players of today. Whereas 25 years ago recorder playing in schools was generally confined to the older children, today excellent playing is being achieved by the six- and seven-year olds in the Infant schools.

Also available for the first time are books of pianoforte accompaniments for each of *The School Recorder Books*. Further information about these is given at the end of the introduction.

We wish to express our thanks to the many people who have helped in this revision and particularly to the late Mr. B. W. Appleby, M.B.E., M.A., formerly Organiser of Music, Doncaster, and to the many publishers who have allowed the use of their copyright material.

COPYRIGHT

EDMUND PRIESTLEY
FRED FOWLER

Frontispiece from an instruction book for the recorder, published in 1683

Introduction

MEN AND MUSIC

Henry VIII became King of England in 1509. He was a fine musician. Not only did he compose songs and church music, but he was also a skilful performer on several instruments of the time. He could play the virginal, or piano of that day, the lute, the flute and, more interesting to us, the recorder. He had a great collection of instruments, no less than seventy-six of them being recorders.

Much of the music in the sixteenth century consisted of choral singing without accompaniment. There were no orchestras as we know them. The fore-runners of the modern violins, called viols, were very popular, and combined in groups, or "chests", very much like our modern string quartets. In a similar manner the different types of recorders combined to play together, and were known as "consorts of recorders".

Nearly one hundred years after Henry VIII ascended the throne, Shakespeare was writing his plays, and in one of them, *Hamlet*, he not only mentions the recorder, but brings it on to the stage in full view of the audience, and makes his characters talk about it, its music, its construction, and how it is played. Shakespeare also mentions the recorder in Act V of *A Midsummer Night's Dream*, and during the performance of his plays recorders were used to provide some of the incidental music, particularly when the scene was quiet, religious, or mournful.

Our third historical figure, Samuel Pepys, lived at the time of the Great Plague and the Great Fire of London in 1665 and 1666. Perhaps many beautiful recorders, skilfully made by hand in the music-shops of the City, were destroyed. Even if this were the case, we know from the writings of this man that such shops were soon going about their business as usual. Samuel Pepys became Clerk of the King's ships in 1660, and he kept a diary from that year until 1669. It is still in existence and is valuable because of the fine picture it gives of London life and people in the years of the Restoration. Pepys heard some recorders at the theatre and was so pleased with their sweetness that he decided to learn to play one himself. Hence this entry in his diary:

> April 8, 1668, "To Drumbleby's and did there talk a great deal about pipes, and did buy a recorder which I do intend to learn to play on, the sound of it being of all sounds in the world, most pleasing to me."

A few years after Pepys had made this entry in his diary, George Frederick Handel was born (1685). There is no need to tell you how famous he became as a

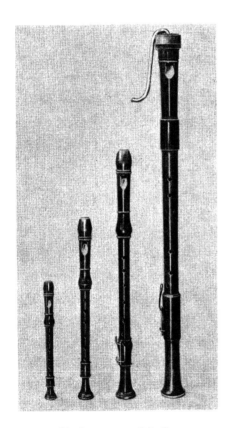

The Instruments of the Consort
(Descant, Treble, Tenor and Bass)

musician, for you will all be familiar with some of his music, his *Largo*, his *Water Music*, or his *Messiah*. We are mentioning Handel because he was one of the many famous composers who wrote music for the recorder. His sonatas for the treble recorder are often performed nowadays, but the recorder is no longer used in his oratorios as he intended it to be. In *See the conqu'ring hero comes* from *Judas Maccabeus*, he used the modern flute, but for the quieter *Wise men flattering may deceive you*, he found the recorder more suitable.

Thus the recorder is connected with four great figures. In 1509, when the first of these ascended the English throne, recorders were becoming very popular in this country and on the continent. They were, of course, often played before that time, and there is in existence a picture of a recorder player dating back to 1175. The period of their popularity, however, dates roughly from 1500 to 1700, and by the time Handel died, in 1759, interest in them, was declining, and a hundred years later they were almost forgotten.

The chief reason for their disappearance lies in the growth of the orchestra. The playing together of different types of instruments was almost unknown in the time of Henry VIII, but the modern orchestra was beginning to take shape by the time of Handel. It was found that the fuller tone of the modern flute combined better with other instruments than the quieter tone of the recorder. Thus for more than a century recorders were unknown and people forgot the art of making them. Now they have been rediscovered, and the instrument that you are learning to play is very similar to those which Henry VIII played, Pepys admired, Shakespeare described in his plays, and Handel employed in his music. This present revival of recorder making and playing is chiefly due to the work of the late Mr. Arnold Dolmetsch, and we owe him a great debt for his research into the music and instruments of former times.

The photograph on page 5 shows the four principal sizes of the recorder which are played today. From left to right you see the descant, treble, tenor and bass instruments. The descant, treble and tenor have a range of more than two octaves, whilst the range of the bass is slightly less. The lowest note of the descant recorder, that is the note played when all the holes are covered, is the C above the middle C on the piano. The lowest note of the treble is the F above middle C. The tenor is one octave lower than the descant and so its lowest note is middle C. The bass recorder is one octave lower than the treble and its lowest note, therefore, is the F below middle C on the piano. Music for the descant and bass recorders is written an octave lower than it sounds in order to avoid excessive use of leger lines.

THE CARE OF YOUR RECORDER

Your recorder is either made of wood or plastic, and consists of two or three separate parts. When joining the parts together or separating them always use a screwing motion. If you just "pull or push" you might crack the instrument.

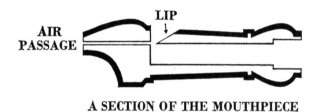

A SECTION OF THE MOUTHPIECE

The most delicate part of the recorder is the mouthpiece which contains the narrow air passage (see above). Your breath goes through this and, hitting the sharp edge called the "lip", sets up vibrations. If the sharp edge is damaged your instrument is useless. When the air passage becomes blocked by dirt never use anything hard such as a knife or a needle to clean it out, for you may touch the "lip" and damage it. Always use something soft such as the tip of a feather. If moisture collects in the air passage, blow down it whilst covering the lip with a finger. In this way the moisture is removed silently.

In addition to the mouthpiece, your recorder consists of a tube with finger holes. This tube is made in one or two pieces. Quite often moisture collects in the tube when you play. If your recorder is a wooden one it is very important that you should dry the tube after you finish playing. For this purpose use a "pull through", made of a small piece of soft material tied to a length of string. The tube of a wooden recorder should be oiled lightly every few months. Use a "pull through" rag to which a small quantity of oil has been added, or use a brush made specially for this purpose by the recorder manufacturers, who also supply the correct type of oil.

The joints of the various parts are generally wrapped with waxed thread. If the joints fit loosely after a time just scratch the thread lightly with your finger nail. If the waxed thread eventually comes off, re-wrap with thin thread or cotton, but do not use too much or you might split the instrument. On some recorders the joints are covered with cork. If this wears away in time, new cork rings may be obtained from the makers.

Wooden recorders should never be kept in a hot place or exposed to the sun.

Some recorder manufacturers supply "spare parts", so that if you break one part of your instrument you do not have to buy another complete recorder.

THE NOTE-SEQUENCE OF THIS BOOK

Pages 8–19	Five left-hand notes—B, A, G, C¹ and D¹	
Pages 20–24	Introducing the right-hand—F♯, E and D	
Pages 25–27	A 'pinched' note—	E¹
Pages 28–32	Further use of the right-hand— F and C	
Pages 33–34	The introduction of a flat—	B♭
Pages 35–38	Three higher notes— F¹, F♯¹ and G¹	

Piano Accompaniments

Two books of piano accompaniments, one for each of the revised editions of *The School Recorder Books* 1 and 2, have been made available so that teachers do not have to refer to several books to find all the accompaniments they need. The piano, provided it is at new philharmonic pitch (C 522), should frequently be used with beginners as it helps them to play in tune. The books contain all accompaniments that are likely to be required for the tunes in *The School Recorder Books*. At the head of each piece of music in these *Books of Piano Accompaniments* there is a page reference to the appropriate tune in *The School Recorder Book* whilst, in the latter, at the end of each relevant piece of music the abbreviation PIANO ACC. is printed: these cross references should prove useful and time-saving.

These books have been published in response to considerable demand and their value to teachers of the recorder will be immediately apparent.

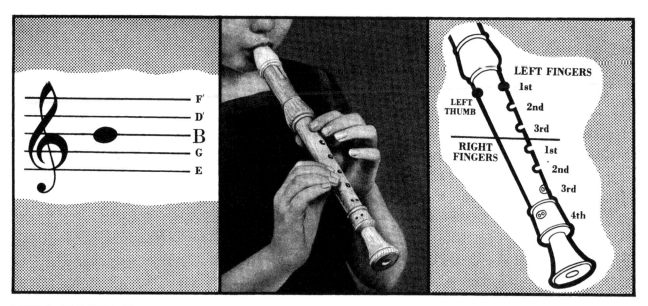

THE NOTE B

We are going to begin by playing the note called B.

The first diagram shows that it is written on the middle line, and the photograph and second diagram show you the fingering. A hole covered by a finger is shown ●.

Hold the recorder well up, with the tip between your lips. Your lips should be covering your teeth, and your teeth should never touch the recorder.

Now look at the position of the hands:

LEFT HAND   Thumb covering the hole at the back.
                   First finger, quite flat, covering the hole nearest your mouth.

RIGHT HAND   Thumb supporting the recorder underneath, just about where you will need it later when you use your right hand fingers.

EXERCISES   Blow very gently and you should play the note B.

Next play the note B several times, saying 'te' each time ('te' as in 'term'). This is known as 'tongueing'. Now play four short B's and one long one as below:

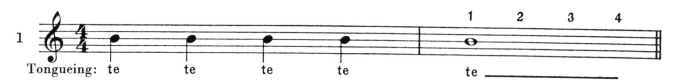

●. or ♩ is a one-beat note (crotchet)   ρ or ♩ is a two-beat note (minim)

ρ. or ♩. is a three-beat note (dotted minim)   o is a four-beat note (semibreve)

$\frac{2}{4}$ $\frac{3}{4}$ etc. at the beginning of the music is called the Time Signature.

$\frac{2}{4}$ means two crotchet beats in a bar, $\frac{3}{4}$ means three crotchet beats in a bar.

What does $\frac{4}{4}$ mean?

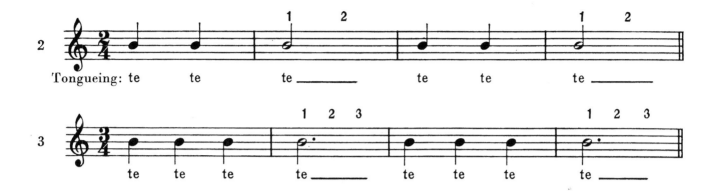

You will find that you will always play an exercise better if you say it and clap it first. Clap one for a crotchet, and two for a minim etc.

This exercise is nearly like exercise number 3 above. Find where it differs before you play it.

This exercise has ♩ in it. The sign ♩ , sometimes written ↾ , means a one-beat (crotchet) rest.

REMEMBER   The tip of the recorder between the lips.
The lips covering the teeth.
Blow very gently and tongue (te) each note.
Keep the fingers flat. Do not try to cover the holes with the *tips* of the fingers.

9

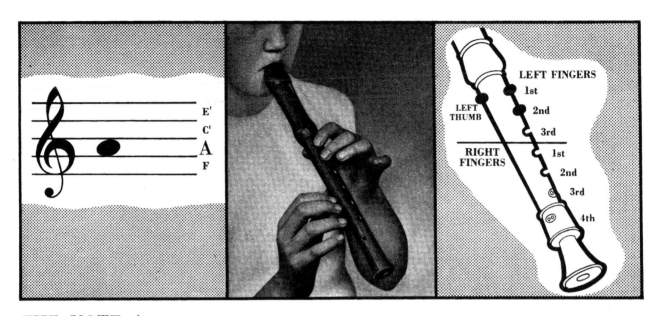

THE NOTE A

This note is in the second space up (see first diagram above).

The photograph and the second diagram show us:

LEFT HAND   Thumb still covering the hole at the back. First and second fingers covering the top two holes at the front.

RIGHT HAND   As before, supporting the instrument.

EXERCISES   Now play four short A's and a long one.

Are your fingers flat on the holes?

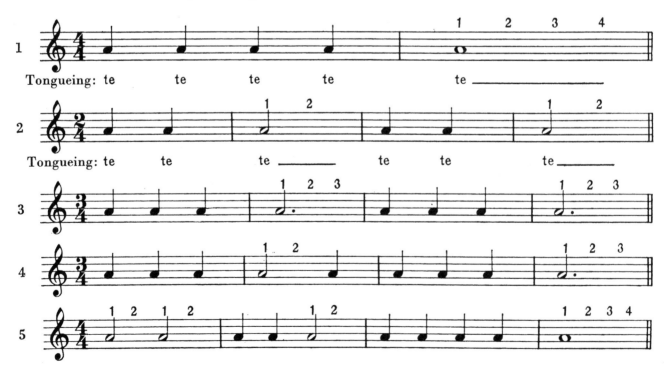

REMEMBER Keep your fingers flat on the holes; blow gently and tongue each note; read the exercises before playing them.

You will remember playing four short B's and a long one and, later, four short A's and a long one.

Here they are together.

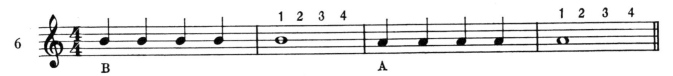

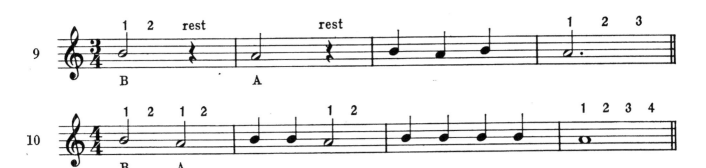

When you lift a finger from a hole do not lift it more than a quarter of an inch. It is then ready to cover the hole again quickly.

The five lines on which our music is written are called the Staff or the Stave. The sign you see at the beginning   is the Treble clef.

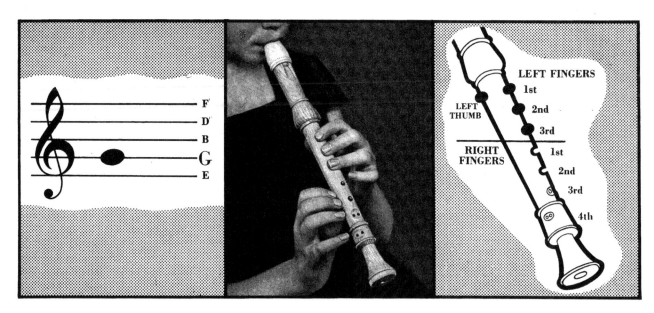

THE NOTE G

G is on the second line up. The fingering is like that for the last note A, with the next left-hand finger added.

LEFT HAND   The first, second and third fingers covering the top three holes. The thumb covering the hole at the back.

RIGHT HAND   Still supporting.

EXERCISES   Blow softly and tongue each note. Remember to hold your recorder well up and to keep your shoulders back.

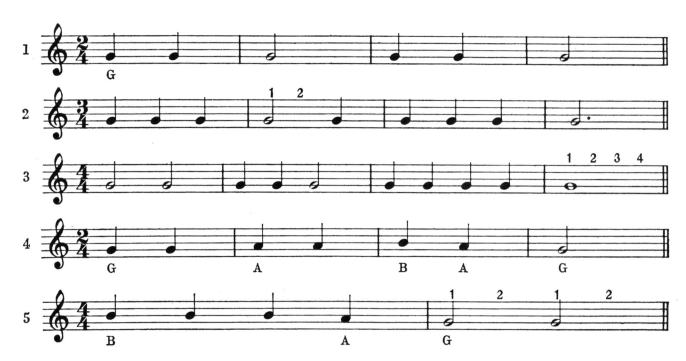

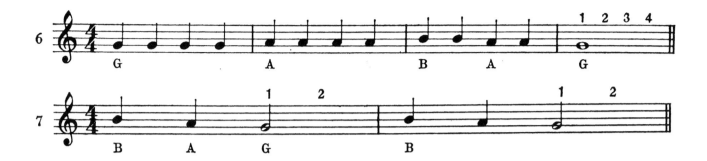

This exercise is very similar to the one above. Do you see the difference? Two of the notes are joined together. ♫ They are quavers, or half beats, and so they are played quicker. Tongue both of them.

Do you know this tune?

REMEMBER to read and clap these exercises before playing them.

This exercise is similar to number 10, but it has some quavers in.

Two quavers to begin with.

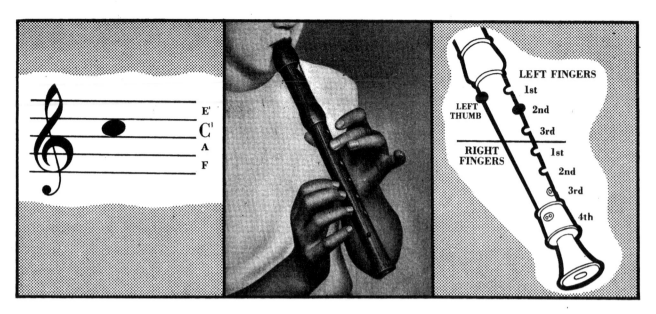

THE NOTE C' (Upper C)

The new note is shown in the third space up (see first diagram above). Now look at the photograph and the second diagram for the fingering.

LEFT HAND   Thumb still on the hole at the back.
The middle finger on the second hole from the top.
Imagine you are going to play A and then lift the first finger.

RIGHT HAND   Still supporting the recorder.

EXERCISES   Remember to say and clap the exercises first.

Clap 1 for a crotchet ♩   2 for a minim ♩
3 for a dotted minim ♩.   4 for a semibreve 𝅝

Now C' and B

Chant (Pelham Humphrey)

PIANO ACC.

14

is a minim (two-beat) rest.

Have you remembered the crotchet (one-beat) rest?......

Now, exercise **9** again, with some quick notes (quavers) in:

Pease pudding hot, *Pease pudding cold,* *Pease pudding in the pot. Nine days old.*

More half beats.

REMEMBER   Your recorder should be held well up—*not* pointing to your feet.
Your shoulders held back.
Do not try to read music with your book on your lap.

Are you remembering to tongue each note (te) and to read and clap the exercises before playing them?

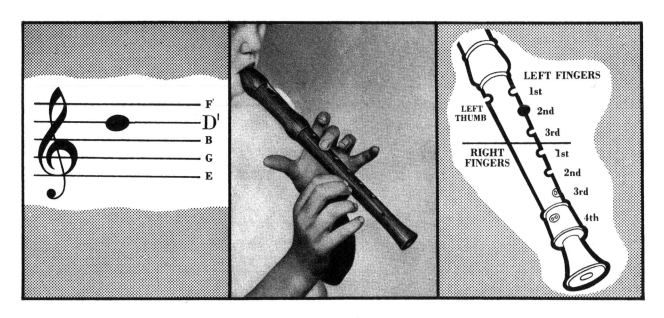

THE NOTE D' (Upper D)

This note is on the fourth line up (see first diagram above). Look at the photograph. What do you notice about the left-hand thumb?

LEFT HAND   Middle finger on the hole next to the top.
Thumb *not* covering the hole at the back.

RIGHT HAND   Still supporting the recorder.

REMEMBER   C' and D' have similar fingerings.
Left-hand thumb ON the hole for C' and OFF for D'—but only about ¼ inch off. So that you can see it is not covering the hole, the left hand thumb has been dropped much too far in the photograph.

EXERCISES

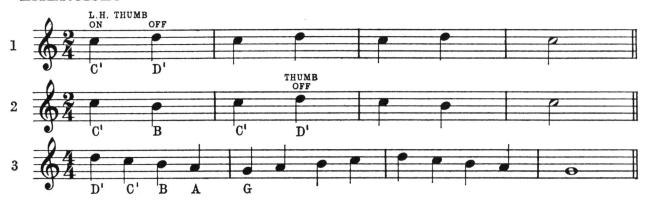

TUNES TO PLAY. Breathing places are indicated √

(*By permission of J. Curwen & Sons Ltd.*)

A tune with a lot of half beats ♪♩ (quavers) in:

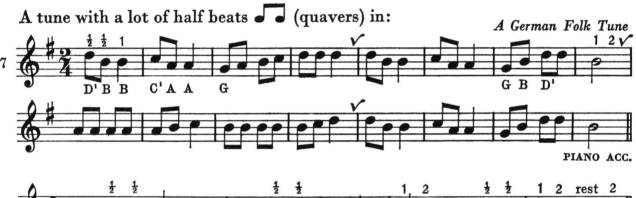

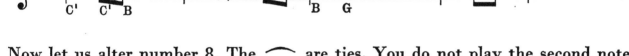

Now let us alter number 8. The ⌒ are ties. You do not play the second note when two notes are tied ♩⌢♩, but hold it on.

It makes the first note 1½ beats (crotchet and quaver tied).
This is another way of writing it:
♩. dotted crotchet is 1½ beats. ♪ quaver is half a beat.

Did you recognise this as the beginning of "All Through The Night"?

ROUND THE CLOCK

A Suite of four short pieces for Descant Recorder and Piano by E. J. Stapleton.
The recorder part only uses the notes G A B C¹ D¹.

Read and clap the tunes before playing them.

ROUND THE CLOCK—Notes on Performance

(1) WAKE UP

We have already met a note with a dot after it (𝅘𝅥. dotted crotchet). A dot after a note makes the note half as long again. We are now going to meet some notes with a dot above or below. This means that such notes have to be played staccato, or cut short. To do this say 'tut' when tongueing, instead of 'te'. All notes which do not have a dot above or below must be given their full value.

(2) BEDTIME

Play quietly and smoothly. Watch the tied notes.

The curved line 'ties' the two G's together and instead of playing each note for 3 beats we play one long G and hold it for 6 beats.

(3) SWINGING

We are now going to play 'slurred' notes.

In recorder playing when there is a curved line between two *different* notes, it means that we tongue the first note but not the second. Just go on blowing and change the fingering as in the following exercise which you should practise.

All notes to be 'tongued' are marked with a 't' in number 3 opposite.

(4) PLAYTIME

In this tune there are examples of three notes covered by the 'slur'.
Only tongue the first note of each group.
Practise this exercise first, and then make an exercise of bars 3 and 4 in the tune.

Very young players may omit the 'slurring' but must not, of course, omit observing any notes which are 'tied'. As soon as possible, however, players should master the 'slur', as it is an important means of expression in recorder playing.

19

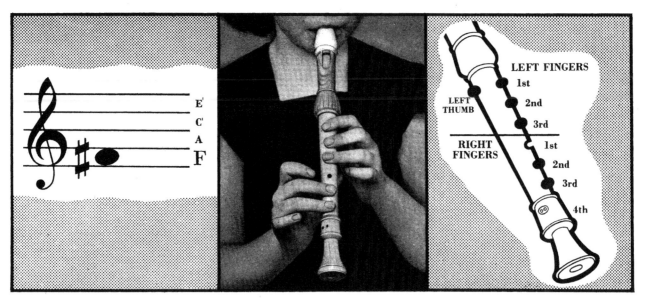

THE NOTE F♯ (F Sharp)

The first of the four spaces is F. The diagram on the left shows you F with a sharp (♯) sign in front of it—F sharp. For the first time we are going to use our right-hand fingers. Look carefully at the photograph and the diagram on the right.

LEFT HAND Fingering as for the note G, including the thumb on the hole at the back.

RIGHT HAND The *middle* two fingers on the *middle* two holes. Keep the fingers flat.

EXERCISES

The sharp sign (♯) is not generally written before each note, but placed at the beginning of the piece of music on the top line, which is also an F (E G B D¹ F¹). This makes *every* F into F♯.

A TUNE TO PLAY. Watch the quavers.

The sign ⌢ means you can hold that note a little longer if you wish.

D. C. al fine means that you repeat this tune from the beginning as far as the word 'Fine' (Finish).

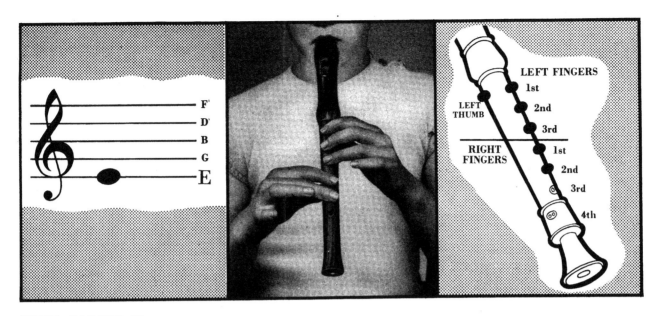

THE NOTE E

E is the note on the first or bottom line.

LEFT HAND   Fingering as for G.

RIGHT HAND   The first and second fingers on the top two right-hand holes.

REMEMBER   The top two right-hand fingers for E,
the middle two right-hand fingers for F♯.

EXERCISES   Notice the sharp sign at the beginning of each line (Key Signature). This makes each F into F♯.

TWO TUNES TO PLAY.

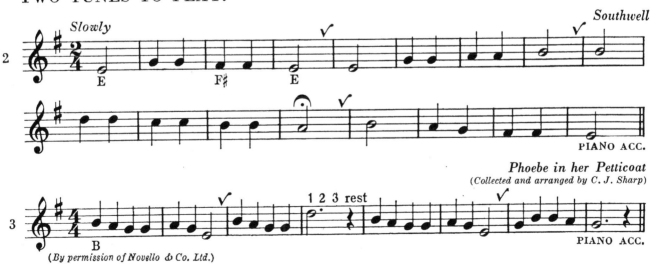

Southwell

PIANO ACC.

Phoebe in her Petticoat
(Collected and arranged by C. J. Sharp)

PIANO ACC.

(By permission of Novello & Co. Ltd.)

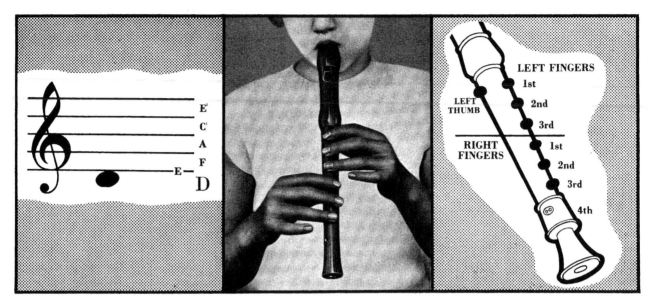

THE NOTE D

The bottom line is for note E, so our new note D is in the space just below. We have previously learnt a note D but that was upper D (D') on the fourth line.

Now look at the photograph and the second diagram for the fingering.

LEFT HAND   Thumb on the hole at the back. The first, second and third fingers on the holes at the front.

RIGHT HAND   First, second and third fingers on the holes leaving just the bottom hole uncovered.

If your recorder has two small holes for the right-hand third finger instead of one larger one, be sure you cover them BOTH.

REMEMBER to keep your fingers flat. Blow gently and tongue each note.

EXERCISES

In the following exercises and tunes there is one sharp (F♯) in the Key Signature.

TUNES TO PLAY   Read and clap them first.

Part Playing   A Canon

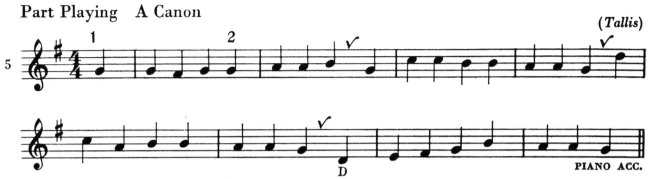

Learn this tune and then divide into two groups. Group 1 begins.
When they reach figure 2 above, group 2 begins playing *from the beginning*.

✓ is a breathing place. (✓) is a place where a breath could be taken but only if absolutely necessary.

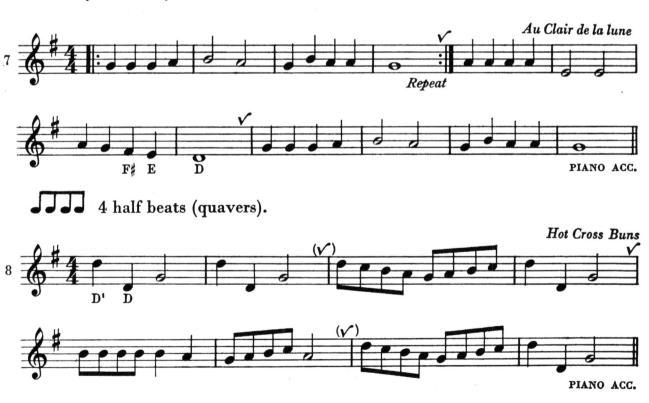

23

Part Playing   A Round

When you can play this tune well, divide into four groups and play it as a round.
You may each finish in turn or together on the notes marked *.

Copyright—reprinted from *Songs of Praise* (*Enlarged Edition*)
by permission of the Oxford University Press

Slurred notes ♩♩ only tongue the first of the two notes.

When you go back to the beginning play as far as the word 'Fine'.
Do *not* repeat the line *this* time.

Part Playing   Another Round

Four groups again.

24

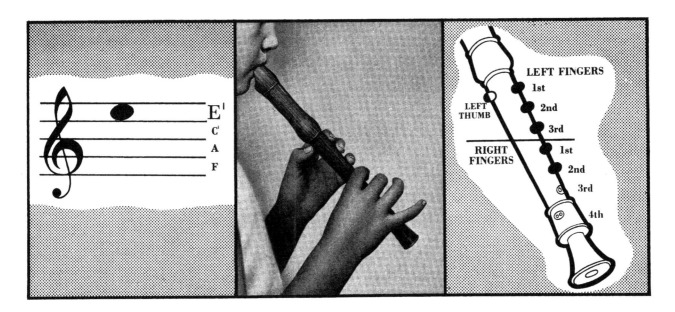

THE NOTE E¹ (Upper E)

We have already learnt the note E (bottom line). Upper E is in the top space, and it is our first "pinched note". In the photograph above, the recorder is turned to show what is meant by a "pinched note". The left-hand thumb does not entirely cover the hole at the back. Instead the thumb nail is pressed into the hole, leaving a small part at the top of the hole uncovered. Apart from this the fingering is the same as lower E (see photograph). In the diagram a pinched note is shown ◖

EXERCISES   Revision of lower E. Thumb covering the hole at the back.

Upper E. Now bend the thumb so that the nail presses into the hole, leaving just a small part of it uncovered.

Now combine Exercises 1 and 2: E E¹ E E¹ E E¹ E.
Practise this until you can play upper E quietly. Tongue each note.

Make up further exercises in which upper E is approached from different notes, e.g.

Number 5 needs a lot of practice, because the left-hand thumb is not covering the hole for D¹.

The Holly and the Ivy
(Collected and arranged by C. J. Sharp)

PIANO ACC.

(*By permission of Novello & Co. Ltd.*)

At first in your eagerness to play upper E you will most probably play it too loudly. Now try to play it quietly and sweetly, in tune. Note the slurs.

All Through the Night

PIANO ACC.

Practise B–E' before playing this.

Richmond

PIANO ACC.

The National Anthem

PIANO ACC.

In order to play "pinched notes" well, the left-hand thumb nail should be neither too long nor too short.

The Sandman (Brahms)

PIANO ACC.

In this tune you will meet  is a dotted quaver ($\frac{3}{4}$ beat) and a semi-quaver ($\frac{1}{4}$ beat). Hold the dotted quaver a little longer than a quaver and make the semi-quaver very short.

Loch Lomond

PIANO ACC.

Notice ♪ ၇ in the following tune—a quaver followed by a quaver rest. That is a half beat note followed by a half beat rest and played like a staccato crotchet (♩).

A German Folk Tune

PIANO ACC.

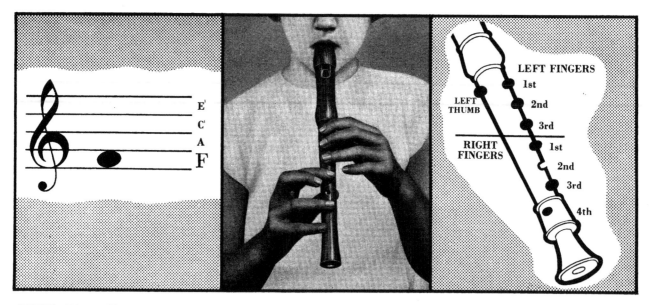

THE NOTE F

We have already played the note F♯. It was the note in the first space, with a sharp sign (♯) either just in front of it or at the beginning of the line of music.

Now we are going to play the same note without the sharp. It is just called F.

Look carefully at the fingering in the photograph and the second diagram.

LEFT HAND   Fingering as for G, with the thumb covering the hole at the back. This is not a "pinched note".

RIGHT HAND   There are four holes for the four fingers. Cover all the holes except that for the second ('middle') finger.

If your recorder is one made of three parts, the lowest part may be turned so that the position of the hole is just right for your little finger. If there are two small holes for the right-hand little finger, cover them BOTH.

EXERCISES   Try to play this note F, blowing and tonguing very gently. If you are not successful do *not* take the recorder from your mouth, but move your fingers until you can feel them covering the holes. Remember—very flat fingers.

When you have played F, raise your right-hand fingers about a quarter of an inch, then lower them and play the note again. For example:

Now try the notes G and F, but before you play the first note G, find F and raise your right-hand fingers so that they are ready to drop when required.

28

Now make up some exercises in which the note F is approached from different notes, e.g.

TUNES TO PLAY   Read and clap them first.

Practise B–F before playing this, and observe the slurs.

Although this tune has F sharp in the Key Signature, you will notice that each time the note F comes it has a natural (♮) sign in front of it, making the note F and not F♯.

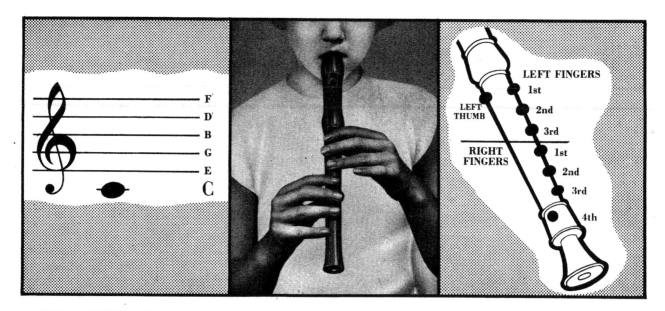

THE NOTE C

This is the lowest note on your recorder. You will remember playing the note D in the space below the bottom line. C is the note below D and so it is on a small line of its own.

From the photograph and the second diagram you will see that all the holes are covered, including the hole at the back. This note requires very gentle blowing and tonguing. If you do not play it correctly at first, do not remove the recorder from your mouth, but move your fingers; keep them flat, feel for the holes and blow and tongue very gently.

EXERCISES From F to C. This just requires the movement of the right-hand middle finger. Fingers flat!

From D to C. This just requires the movement of the right-hand little finger.

Repeated C's need very gentle tonguing.

30

Now start on the lowest note and play up the scale.

Make up exercises in which C is approached from different notes. For example:

TUNES TO PLAY

Monkland

Darwall's 148th

Bamberg

Part Playing   A Round. Very gentle tonguing.

Turn Again Whittington

In the following tune we meet the $\frac{6}{8}$ time signature.

$\frac{6}{8}$ means 6 quavers in a bar, grouped in threes—

At first count 123, 456 in each bar. Count 2 for a crotchet and 3 for a dotted crotchet

Jack and Jill

Jack and Jill went up the hill, to fetch a pail of wat - er;

Jack fell down, and broke his crown, and Jill came tum - bling af - ter.

PIANO ACC.

31

The Harp that once through Tara's Halls

12

PIANO ACC.

Cader Idris

13

PIANO ACC.

$\frac{6}{8}$ time again. At first count 6 in a bar. For ♩.♫ count 1 2 and 3

A German Tune

14

6 1 2 and 3 4 5 6 1 2 3 4 5 6 1 2 3 4 5 6

tied

PIANO ACC.

Part Playing   A longer round.

Slaves to the World

15

When you can play this tune well, divide into three groups and play it as a round.
Finish all together on the notes marked ✳.
The C at the beginning means Common time ($\frac{4}{4}$).

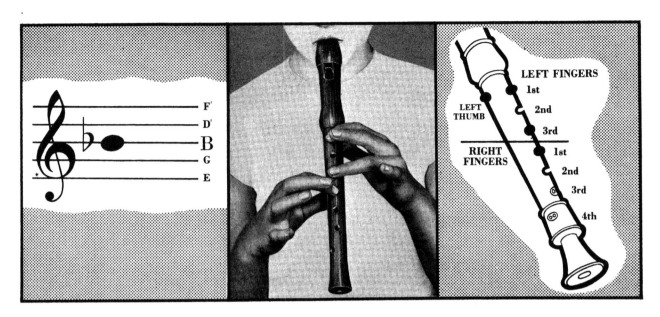

THE NOTE B♭ (B Flat)

The first note we played was B (middle line). The diagram on the left shows you B with a flat (♭) sign in front of it—B flat.

Look carefully at the fingering.

LEFT HAND　　As for note G, but with the middle finger raised. Do not forget the thumb is covering the hole at the back.

RIGHT HAND　　First finger covering the top right-hand hole.

EXERCISES　　The flat sign is not generally written before each B, but placed on the middle line at the beginning of the music. (Key Signature).

TUNES TO PLAY　　Remember to read and clap them first.

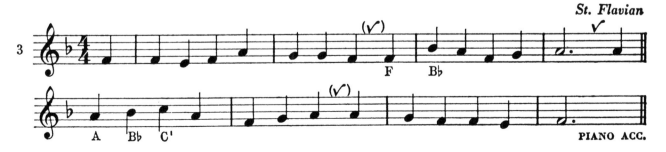

St. Flavian

PIANO ACC.

One note in this tune has a natural (♮) sign in front of it, making it B not B♭.

Winchester Old

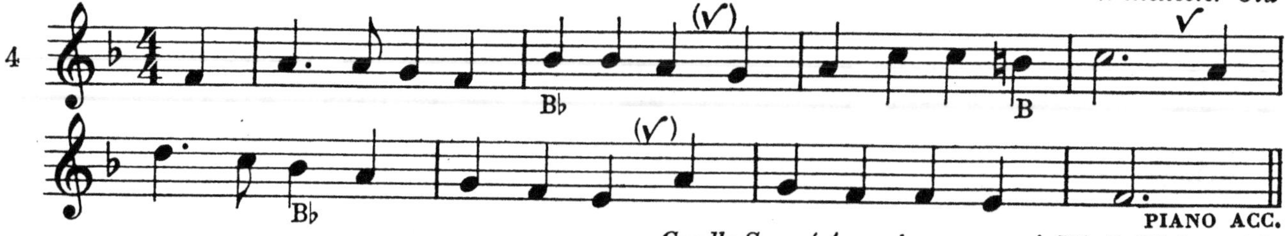

4
(✓)
✓
B♭
B
B♭
(✓)
PIANO ACC.

Cradle Song (Away in a manger) W. J. Kirkpatrick

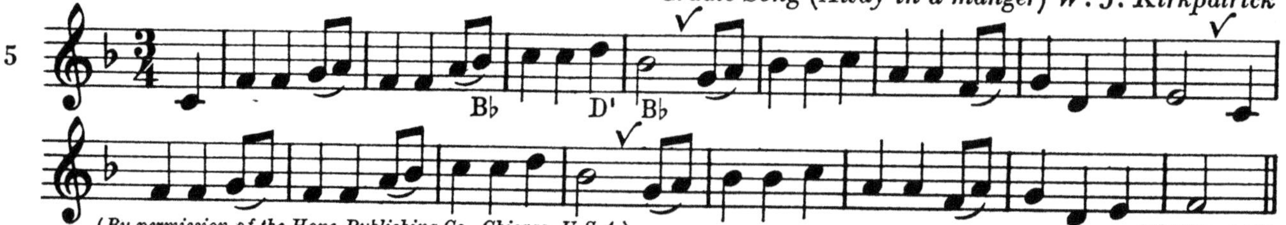

5
✓
✓
B♭
D'
B♭
✓
PIANO ACC.

(By permission of the Hope Publishing Co., Chicago, U.S.A.)

Coventry Carol

6
✓
1 2 3
1 2 3
1 2 ✓
F♯
B♭
✓
1 2 3
B
PIANO ACC.

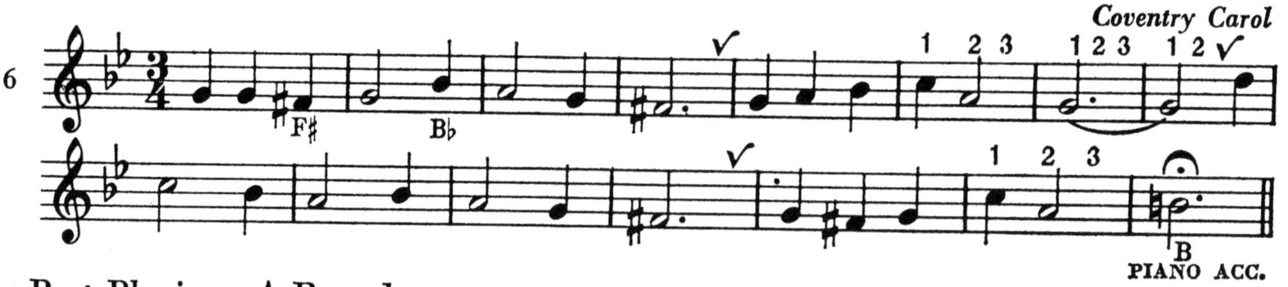

Part Playing A Round.

Frère Jacques

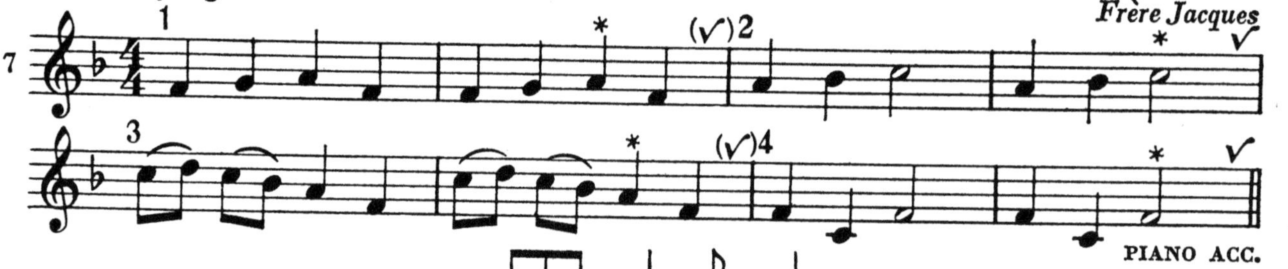

1
7
*
(✓)2
*
✓
3
*
(✓)4
*
✓
PIANO ACC.

6/8 time again. Count
1 2 3
1 2 3
1 2 3

I saw three ships

8
✓
B♭
B♭
PIANO ACC.

Cuckoo (Austrian Folk Song)

9
1✓2 3 and
✓
✓
(✓)
✓
(✓)
PIANO ACC.

By permission of the Assoc. for Childhood Educ. International,
3615, Wisconsin Avenue, N.W., Washington 16, D.C.
from "Songs Children Like", 'Cuckoo' page 11, C 1954 & 1958

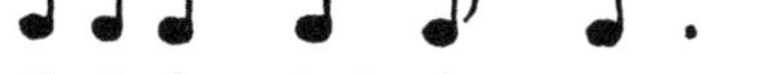

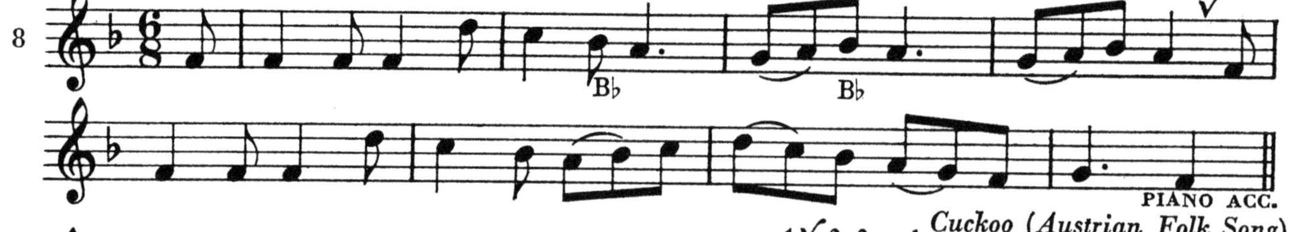

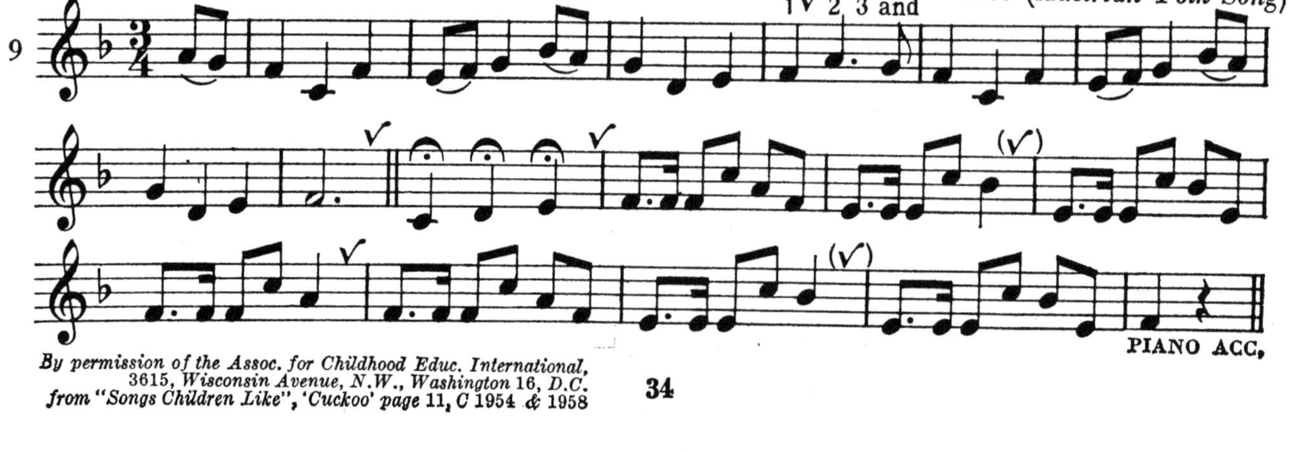

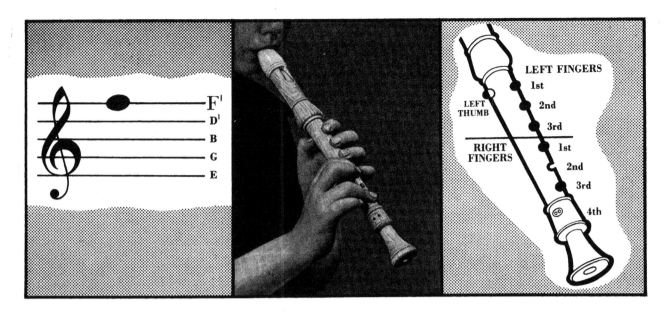

THE NOTE F' (Upper F)

This note is shown on the top line and, like Upper E, it is a "pinched note". The left-hand thumb nail is pressed into the hole at the back, leaving a small part at the top of the hole uncovered. Apart from this, the fingering is the same as for the lower F, except that the RIGHT-HAND LITTLE FINGER does not cover the bottom hole. Compare the fingering for upper F above with that of F on page 28.

EXERCISES Revision of lower F. Thumb covering the hole at the back. All the holes on the front of the recorder covered except that for the right-hand second (middle) finger, see page 28.

Upper F. Lift the right-hand little finger. 'Pinch' the left-hand thumb into the hole at the back.

Exercises 1 and 2 combined. The only movement is that of the left-hand thumb and the right-hand little finger.

TUNES TO PLAY

Will ye no' come back again?

F¹ E¹   B♭

PIANO ACC.

Early one morning

B♭   B♭   F¹

PIANO ACC.

3 and 1 2 and 3   1 rest   Lullaby (Brahms)

F¹   B♭

F F F¹

PIANO ACC.

A Country Dance.

Goddesses

B♭

F¹

PIANO ACC.

Part Playing   Two Rounds.

White Sand

Come, follow

36

THE NOTE F#' (Upper F#)

The last note we played was upper F on the top line. A sharp sign in front of upper F or at the beginning of the music on the top line makes the note upper F sharp. This is another 'pinched note'. Look carefully at the fingering in the photograph above.

EXERCISES

F# and Upper F#.
Left-hand thumb on the hole for F#, but 'pinched' into it for F#'.
Right-hand second and third fingers used for F# (see page 20).
Lift the right-hand third finger when playing F#'.

A TUNE TO PLAY.

The Frog and the Crow

PIANO ACC.

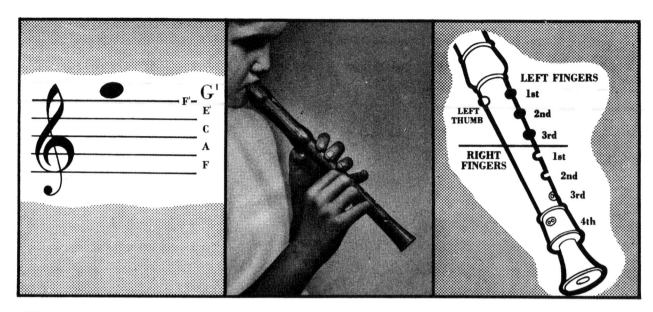

THE NOTE G¹ (Upper G)

The note upper G is shown in the space above the top line (F¹). The fingering is the same as for the lower G (page 12) except that the left-hand thumb is 'pinched' into the hole at the back.

EXERCISES This exercise only requires left-hand thumb movement.

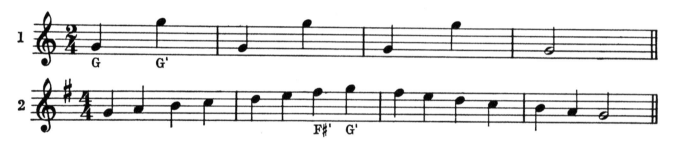

A TUNE TO PLAY In this piece you often get a quaver followed by a quaver rest ♪ 𝄾 This is similar to a staccato crotchet (♩̇)—say 'tut'.

38

Alphabetical Index

The Note-Sequence of
The School Recorder Book Two

THE DESCANT RECORDER

Three sharps	C♯$^|$, G♯ and D♯$^|$
D♯$^|$ by another name	E♭$^|$
Using the "double holes"	D♯ and E♭
New names for familiar fingerings	A♭, D♭$^|$ and A♯
More practice with "double holes"	**C♯ and D♭**
Still higher notes	G♯$^|$, A$^|$, B♭$^|$, B$^|$ and C$^{||}$

THE TREBLE RECORDER

Five left-hand notes	C, D, E, F$^|$ and G$^|$
Introducing the right hand	B, A, G, B♭ and F
A "pinched" note	A$^|$
Two sharps	C♯ and F♯$^|$
Three "pinched" notes	B♭$^|$, B$^|$ and C$^|$
Two flats	E♭ and A♭$^|$
The higher notes	C♯$^|$, D$^|$, E♭$^|$, E$^|$ and F$^{||}$
Using the "double holes"	A♭ (G♯) and G♭ (F♯)